P9-DFM-506

CREEPY CREATURES

ZOMBIES

Big Buddy Books
An Imprint of Abdo Publishing
abdopublishing.com

abdopublishing.com

Published by Abdo Publishing, a division of ABDO, PO Box 398166, Minneapolis, Minnesota 55439.

Printed in the United States of America, North Mankato, Minnesota.
042015
092015

THIS BOOK CONTAINS
RECYCLED MATERIALS

Cover Photo: ©iStockphoto.com.
Interior Photos: AP Images for Warner Bros. Consumer Products (p. 21); ASSOCIATED PRESS (p. 23); Romano Cagnoni/Getty Images (p. 25); CDC.gov.com (p. 27); Deposit Photos (pp. 7, 13); epa european pressphoto agency b.v./Alamy (p. 23); ©iStockphoto.com (pp. 5, 9, 17, 29, 30); Michael Ochs Archives/Getty Images (p. 22); Alberto E. Rodriquez/Getty Images (p. 20); Ronald Grant Archive/Alamy (p. 15); Shutterstock.com (p. 19); Mireille Vautier/Alamy (p. 11).

Coordinating Series Editor: Rochelle Baltzer
Contributing Editors: Megan M. Gunderson, Bridget O'Brien, Marcia Zappa
Graphic Design: Jenny Christensen

Library of Congress Cataloging-in-Publication Data

Tieck, Sarah, 1976- author.
Zombies / Sarah Tieck.
pages cm. -- (Creepy creatures)
ISBN 978-1-62403-770-2
1. Zombies--Juvenile literature. I. Title.
GR581.T54 2016
398.21--dc23
2015004215

Contents

Creepy Zombies 4
Scary Stories 6
Around the World 10
Living History 14
Good or Evil? 18
Zombies in Pop Culture 20
Fact or Fiction? 24
What Do You Think? 28
Let's Talk 30
Glossary 31
Websites 31
Index 32

Creepy Zombies

People love to tell spooky stories, especially about creepy creatures such as zombies. They describe their rotting flesh and missing body parts. They say zombies groan and eat human brains!

Zombies have appeared in books, stories, plays, television shows, and movies. But are they real, or the stuff of **legend**? Let's find out more about zombies, and you can decide for yourself!

Zombies often rise from the dead. So, they may be wearing the clothes they were buried in.

Scary Stories

People usually think of zombies as the walking dead. Stories describe zombies as moving slowly. Zombies have pale or discolored skin. They might even have wounds or be rotting.

Zombies are not in control of their own minds. Some are created and ruled by magic. Others are created by exposure to **radiation** or catching a sickness.

Most zombies do not have homes. They may roam in pairs or groups.

Since zombies are already dead, they feel no pain. This makes them hard to stop. In some stories, people must cut off a zombie's head or do something to destroy its brain to halt its deadly advance.

If a zombie is controlled by magic, the witch or sorcerer behind it may need to be destroyed to stop the zombie.

Zombies are messy eaters! In stories, they eat brains and drink blood.

Around the World

People from many **cultures** tell stories of zombies or zombie-like creatures. Most stories describe people rising from the dead and taking over the world.

On the island of Haiti, there are folktales about *zombi*. Some people believe zombi are part of **voodoo**. They describe bodies or souls being controlled by magic. This is caused by a **spell** cast by a sorcerer called a *bocor*.

Did you know?

Human skulls, candles, and fire are often part of voodoo rituals.

The Zombies is a painting by voodoo priest Hector Hyppolite of Haiti.

Africa is where zombie stories started. In these stories, people with **supernatural** powers bring back the dead. They force them to work. The zombies can be returned to their graves with salt.

In China, there are stories about hopping zombies. These have features of both vampires and zombies. They are scary and feed on people's life energy. Hopping zombies are also in stories from Korea and Japan.

Zombies are also called flesh-eaters or ghouls.

Living History

Zombie stories go back hundreds of years. Robert Southey was a British writer who lived from 1774 to 1843. He is thought to be the first to use the word *zombie*. In 1819, he used it in *History of Brazil*.

Most people believe modern zombie stories began with the **voodoo** zombi of Haiti. In 1929, William Seabrook printed *The Magic Island*. In it, he describes what he saw on a trip to Haiti. This is one of the first popular books about zombies.

In 1932, a movie based on *The Magic Island* came out. In *White Zombie,* Bela Lugosi plays a sorcerer. He uses his magic to turn people into zombies and control them.

In the 1960s, the modern idea of zombies began appearing in movies. Zombies were not controlled by magic. Instead, they were undead and hungry for human flesh. They usually died when their brains were destroyed.

Zombies remain popular as the focus of video games, movies, TV shows, and books. People also dress up as zombies for special walks or events.

Large groups of people have dressed as zombies and gathered in cities around the world. Called zombie mobs, they do fun things such as dance.

Good or Evil?

In many stories, zombies are monsters to be feared. They may have **supernatural** strength. People have to figure out how to stop them.

In some stories, zombies are misunderstood. They are confused about what has happened to them. Or, maybe they are lonely. Some are even able to find their human feelings again.

Zombies are so strong they can break out of their graves.

ParaNorman

Norman is a boy with special powers. He fights zombies and ghosts to protect his town in the 2012 movie *ParaNorman*.

Did you know?

Zombie Chasers is a popular children's book series. In the books, most of the country becomes sick with a zombie virus. Zack Clarke and his helpers fight back!

Zombies in Pop Culture

Scooby-Doo on Zombie Island

In 1998, the cartoon movie *Scooby-Doo on Zombie Island* came out. In the movie, Scooby-Doo and his friends fight zombies.

Michael Jackson's "Thriller"

In the 1983 music video for this song, zombies rise from their graves. They do a now-famous dance with singer Michael Jackson.

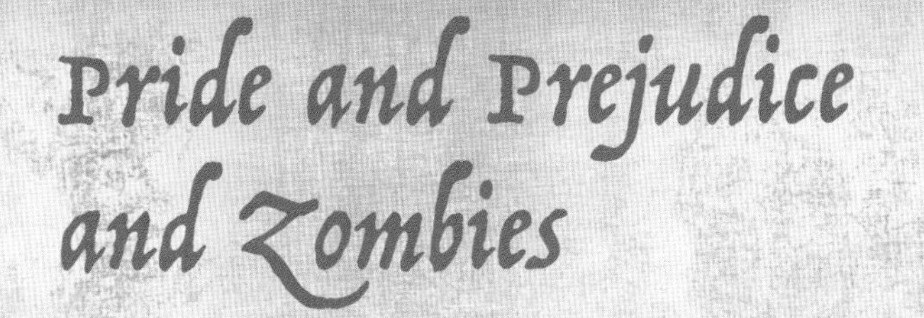

Pride and Prejudice and Zombies

In 2009, author Seth Grahame-Smith rewrote Jane Austen's famous 1813 book, *Pride and Prejudice*. In the new story, the characters fight against zombies.

Plants vs. Zombies

In this video game, plants stop zombies. Each plant has different powers.

Fact or Fiction?

Today, most people don't believe zombies are real. But, some real-life events have made people think the opposite.

Certain **voodoo** activities can cause people to speak or dance without being aware of it. Scientists say this is from drugs or foods used in **rituals**. But for a person watching, it might look like people are zombies.

In some voodoo ceremonies people dress as zombies. Outsiders who do not understand what they are seeing may become afraid.

The idea of a zombie **apocalypse** became popular in the 2000s. Some people believed it was possible. Others had fun imagining it. The US government used this popular interest to teach people about being prepared in case of **disasters**.

To be ready for a disaster, the US government says people should have items such as food, water, money, and tools. They wrote about this in *Preparedness 101: Zombie Pandemic*.

The Centers for Disease Control made posters. It used people's interest in zombies to share real, helpful information about disasters.

What Do You Think?

So, what do you think about zombies? Do they still send a chill up your spine? It can be fun to watch spooky movies about zombies or to dress as a zombie on Halloween.

It is also interesting to learn about zombies. Knowing what is true and what is made up is powerful. Read **fiction** about zombies or look into the real-life history that made people interested in them. Either way, you are in for an exciting journey.

People's ideas about zombies have changed over the years. But, they are still creepy creatures!

Let's Talk

What examples of zombie stories can you think of?

What would you do if you had to fight a zombie?

How do you think it would feel to be a zombie and not be in control of your choices?

Imagine that everyone in the world was a zombie. What do you think would change about how people live?

If you were to write a story about a zombie, what would happen in your story? What **supernatural** powers would your zombie have?

Glossary

apocalypse a sudden, often violent, event that brings great change or destruction.

culture (KUHL-chuhr) the arts, beliefs, and ways of life of a group of people.

disaster (dih-ZAS-tuhr) an event that causes damage and suffering.

fiction stories that are not real.

legend an old story that many believe, but cannot be proven true.

radiation a type of powerful and dangerous energy produced by radioactive material and nuclear reactions.

ritual (RIH-chuh-wuhl) a formal act or set of acts that is repeated.

spell words with magic powers.

supernatural unable to be explained by science or nature.

voodoo a religion that is practiced mostly in Haiti.

To learn more about Creepy Creatures, visit **booklinks.abdopublishing.com**. These links are routinely monitored and updated to provide the most current information available.

Index

Africa **12**

appearance **4, 5, 6**

China **12**

Haiti **10, 11, 14**

History of Brazil **14**

Japan **12**

Korea **12**

magic **6, 8, 10, 15, 16**

Magic Island, The **14, 15**

ParaNorman **20**

Plants vs. Zombies **23**

Preparedness 101: Zombie Pandemic **26**

Pride and Prejudice and Zombies **23**

protection **8, 12, 16, 18**

Scooby-Doo on Zombie Island **21**

"Thriller" **22**

voodoo **10, 11, 14, 24, 25**

White Zombie **15**

zombie apocalypse **26**

Zombie Chasers books **20**

zombie mobs **16, 17**